SALLY RIDE
TAM O'SHAUGHNESSY

VOYAGER

An Adventure
to the Edge
of the
Solar System

Sally Ride Science • San Diego

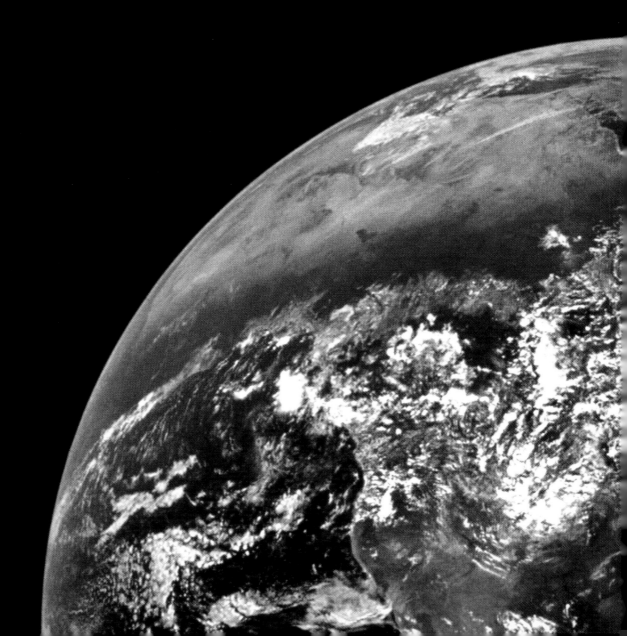

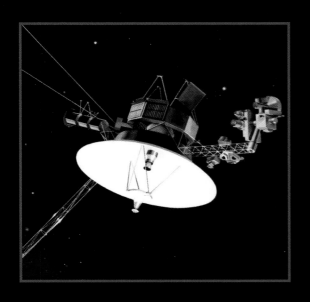

This is the story
of two spacecraft:
Voyager 1 and *Voyager* 2.
They were launched from Earth
to explore four distant planets:
Jupiter, Saturn, Uranus,
and Neptune.

Earth is the third of nine planets that circle the star we call the Sun. Jupiter, Saturn, Uranus, and Neptune are the fifth, sixth, seventh, and eighth planets in our solar system. They are very, very far away. Even when Jupiter is closest to Earth, it is 400 million miles away from us. Neptune is 3 billion miles away.

All four of these planets are very different from Earth. All of them are huge. In fact, they are so big they are called the "giant planets".

None of the giant planets have solid ground to stand on. They are made mostly of hydrogen and helium, the lightest gases in the universe. As you move into the planet the gas gets thicker and thicker, until it is so thick it becomes a liquid or slush.

The first two giant planets, Jupiter and Saturn, are like each other in many ways. Jupiter is the biggest planet in the solar system—more than one thousand Earths would fit inside it! Saturn is nearly as big as Jupiter.

The four giant planets, Jupiter, Saturn, Uranus, and Neptune, shown to scale. Earth (*below*) is also shown to scale.

Uranus and Neptune are also very much alike. They are not as big as Jupiter and Saturn, but both are much, much bigger than Earth. Because they are so far away from the Sun, they are cold, dark planets.

Scientists had studied the four giant planets through telescopes for centuries. They had learned a lot about the planets, but even the most powerful telescopes did not show many details of these distant worlds. Scientists wanted a closer look. They knew that it was impossible to send astronauts that far. Astronauts have never traveled beyond our own moon. A trip to the giant planets would be thousands of times farther and would take several years. But a robotic spacecraft could make the long journey and send back pictures and information to scientists on Earth.

The mission was so important that two spacecraft were built, *Voyager* 1 and *Voyager* 2. Scientists decided to send two spacecraft so that if one broke down on the long trip, there would still be one left.

The *Voyagers* were not very big—each one was about the size of a small car. They would carry special cameras with telescopic lenses to take close-up pictures of the giant planets and their moons. Other instruments would measure ultraviolet and infrared light, invisible to normal cameras, to provide information about the compositions and temperatures of the planets.

During their long trip through space, the *Voyagers* would be controlled from Earth. Scientists would radio commands to the spacecraft telling them what path to follow, what to photograph, and when to send back information. The *Voyagers'* antennas would always be pointed toward Earth, ready to receive instructions.

The pictures and information collected by the spacecraft would be radioed back to Earth. But the *Voyagers'* radio transmitters were not very powerful, and scientists knew that by the time their signals reached Earth they would be very, very weak. Listening for those signals would be like listening for a whisper from thousands of miles away. Several huge radio antennas all over the world would be straining to hear messages from the *Voyagers*.

Mission Control

▶ Radio signals from the *Voyagers* were picked up by large antennas in California, Australia, and Spain. The signals were then relayed by satellite to Mission Control in Pasadena, California.

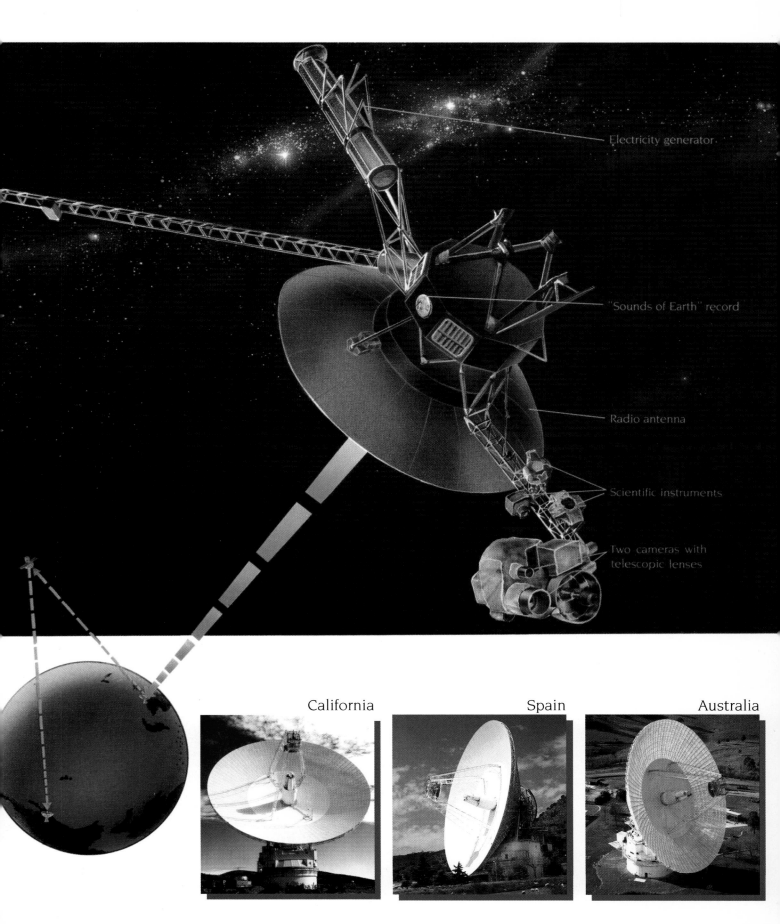

Electricity generator

"Sounds of Earth" record

Radio antenna

Scientific instruments

Two cameras with telescopic lenses

California

Spain

Australia

Exploring all four giant planets is possible only when the planets are in certain places in their orbits around the Sun. When the planets are in these positions, each planet's gravity can be used—like a slingshot—to speed up the spacecraft and send it toward the next planet. The *Voyagers* would fly to Jupiter first, and then use Jupiter's gravity to accelerate them toward Saturn. If both *Voyagers* were still working when they got to Saturn, one spacecraft would be sent to study Saturn's largest moon, Titan, and the other would continue on to explore Uranus and Neptune.

It is very rare for all four giant planets to be in positions that allow one spacecraft to visit all of them. It only happens once every 176 years. The *Voyager* mission was a once-in-a-lifetime opportunity.

▼ Launch

SATURN
NOV. 1980

JUPITER, MAR. 1979

Voyager 1

SATURN
AUG. 1981

JUPITER,
JULY 1979

Voyager 1, LAUNCHED SEPT. 5, 1977

Voyager 2, LAUNCHED AUG. 20, 1977

POSITION OF PLUTO,
AUG. 1989

URANUS, JAN. 1986

NEPTUNE, AUG. 1989

The flight paths of the two *Voyagers*. *Voyager* 1 was launched second but took a faster route to Jupiter. After visiting Saturn, *Voyager* 1 took an upward path out of the solar system. *Voyager* 2 continued to Uranus and Neptune.

Voyager 2

In the summer of 1977, each *Voyager* spacecraft was launched into space by a powerful rocket. Soon they were flying so fast that they passed the Moon in only ten hours. As *Voyager* 1 was speeding away, it looked back to take this picture of the Earth and Moon it was leaving behind.

The two *Voyagers* would have to pass through the asteroid belt on their way to Jupiter. Asteroids are huge rocks that orbit around the Sun. There are thousands of them between Mars and Jupiter, and a collision with one could destroy a spacecraft. Both *Voyagers* made it safely through the asteroid belt. *Voyager* 1 led the way to Jupiter, the first giant planet.

JUPITER

The *Voyagers* sped closer and closer to Jupiter. As the two spacecraft approached the planet, hundreds of scientists crowded into Mission Control to see the close-up pictures of this faraway world.

The radio signals that carried *Voyagers'* pictures travel at the speed of light. So although it had taken the *Voyagers* one and a half years to travel to Jupiter, the photographs traveled back to Earth in only about 45 minutes. The pictures were received by the huge antennas on Earth, then relayed to Mission Control and displayed on big TV screens. The scientists were stunned by what they saw.

Jupiter has bright colors and complex patterns that scientists had never seen through their telescopes. The giant planet is covered with wide bands of yellow, orange, red, and white clouds. Violent storms whipped through the clouds.

The Great Red Spot is a huge storm in Jupiter's atmosphere. Scientists had looked at it through telescopes for over three hundred years, but they had never been able to study its motion. Hundreds of the *Voyagers'* photographs were put together to create a movie of the Great Red Spot. The movie showed the storm swirling swiftly around its center, with hurricane-force winds around its edges.

Each of the smaller white circles is also a fierce, swirling storm. Although the white storms look small next to the Great Red Spot, some of them are as big as the Earth.

Jupiter has many moons that circle around it like a miniature solar system. The *Voyagers* discovered three new moons, and took the first close-up photographs of many others.

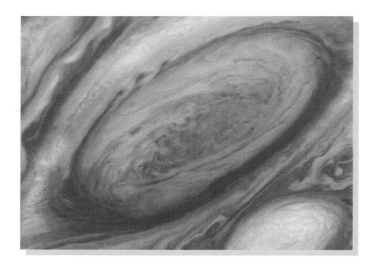

▲ Two pictures of Jupiter's Great Red Spot. The distance from top to bottom in the lower picture is about 15,000 miles.

Jupiter's moon Callisto has been hit by meteorites for over 4 billion years. Each of these collisions left a crater in Callisto's icy surface. Some of the craters look very bright. These are the newer ones. Each collision sprays fresh ice over the surface, and the freshest ice is the brightest.

Long ago, a very big object—maybe an asteroid—crashed into Callisto. The moon's icy ground wasn't strong enough to hold the shape of the huge crater left by the impact. Callisto's surface sagged back to its original shape, and now all that's left is a bright patch of ice and a series of faint rings that formed at the time of the collision.

Callisto

▼ Callisto's surface, showing the enormous bright patch of ice and faint rings left by one huge impact and thousands of craters left by smaller impacts.

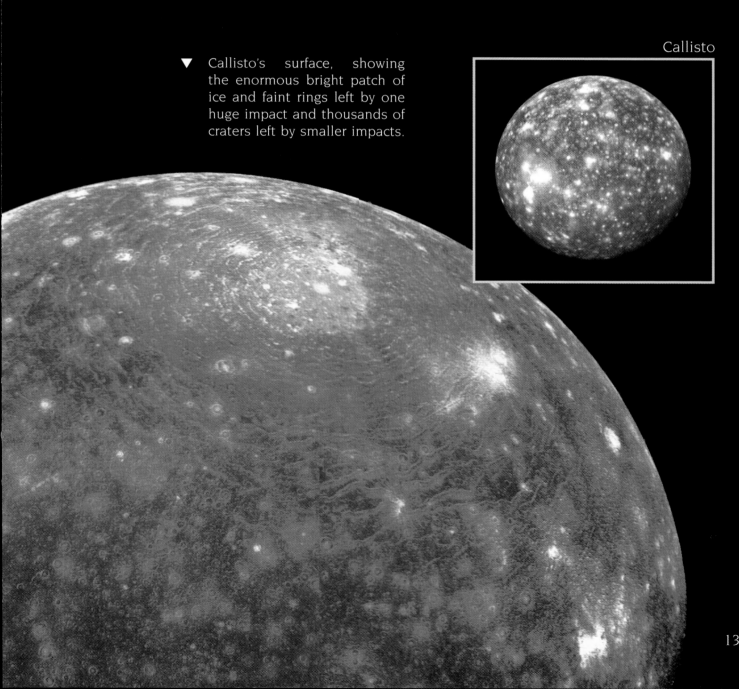

13

Scientists expected most of the moons in the solar system to look like Callisto—dark, frozen, and covered with craters. They were shocked when they saw the pictures of Io, another of Jupiter's moons. There were no craters, and its surface looked orange and splotchy. At first Io was a complete mystery. But then one picture showed something completely unexpected: a volcano erupting! There are active volcanoes on Earth, but scientists did not expect to find them anywhere else in the solar system. Nine volcanoes were erupting on Io while the *Voyagers* flew past, some throwing hot gas hundreds of miles high. There are no craters on Io because lava from the volcanoes flows over its surface and fills in the craters. The cooled lava contains the chemical sulfur, which gives Io its orange, yellow, red, and black colors.

Europa is ice to Io's fire. This moon of Jupiter surprised scientists, too. It is covered with a very smooth, very thick layer of ice. The lines on its surface are cracks in the ice. Fresh ice oozes up through the cracks. Scientists were astonished to learn that there might be a huge ocean beneath Europa's icy crust. Imagine—an enormous ocean of water on a distant moon of Jupiter! Fifteen years later, the *Galileo* spacecraft would confirm this amazing discovery.

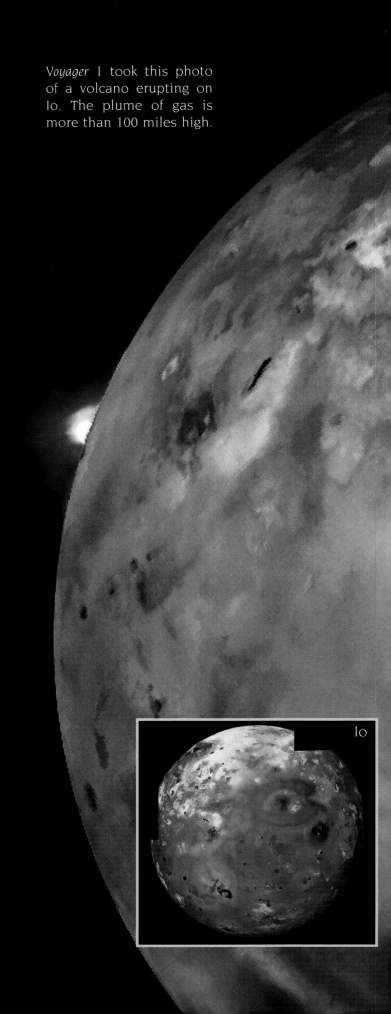

Voyager 1 took this photo of a volcano erupting on Io. The plume of gas is more than 100 miles high.

Io

Like Callisto, Europa has been hit by thousands of meteorites. But there are very few craters left on its surface. Europa's layer of ice must have once been mushy, or even liquid, and erased the craters.

For hundreds of years, scientists thought that Saturn was the only planet with rings. Then the *Voyagers* discovered a thin ring around Jupiter. The ring could not be seen from Earth. Even the *Voyagers'* sensitive cameras could barely make it out.

The ring is made of small dust particles that are circling the planet. But where does the dust come from? The *Voyagers* discovered two tiny moons at the edge of the ring. Scientists think that meteorites hit those moons and knock dust off their surfaces. The dust goes into orbit around the planet and becomes part of the ring.

The *Voyagers* relayed more than 30,000 photographs of Jupiter and its moons back to Earth. As scientists settled down to study the pictures, the twin spacecraft began their two-year trip to the next planet, Saturn.

Europa

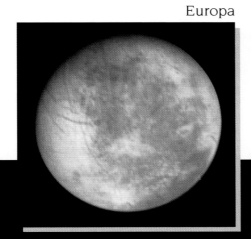

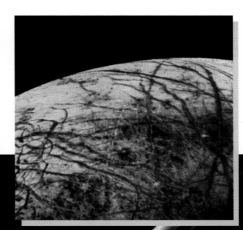

◄ Europa's icy surface, covered with cracks and ridges.

Jupiter's ring (*at the bottom of the picture*), lit by sunlight coming from behind the planet.

SATURN

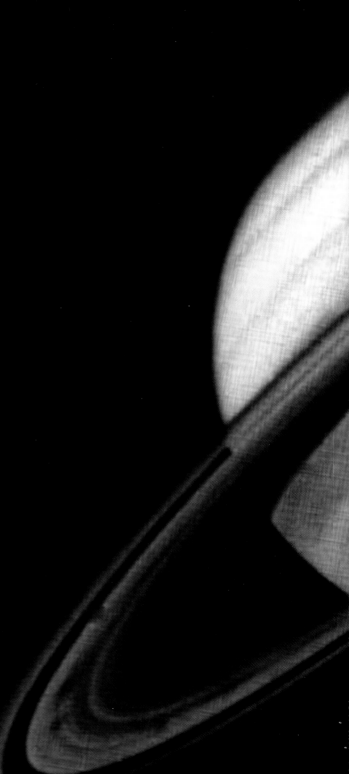

Saturn is the second largest planet in the solar system—only Jupiter is bigger. But although Saturn is big, it is very light. It is not like a big rock. A rock would sink in a bucket of water. If you could find a bucket big enough, Saturn would float in it.

When astronomers looked at Saturn through telescopes on Earth, they saw a yellow, hazy planet with three beautiful rings. But as the *Voyagers* got closer and closer, they showed Saturn as it had never been seen before. The planet had broad belts of brown, yellow, and orange clouds. Its striped atmosphere reminded scientists of Jupiter, but the colors weren't as bright, and the bands weren't as sharp.

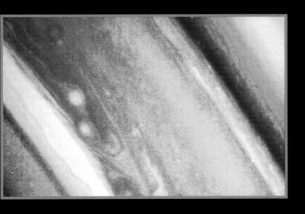

Saturn's atmosphere, photographed by *Voyager* 2. The white band is moving at more than 300 miles per hour. ▶

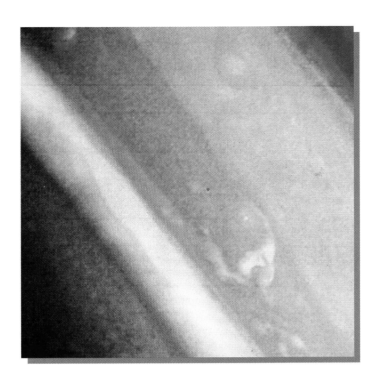

High winds howl through Saturn's atmosphere, blowing much faster than any winds on Earth. Jet streams neat Saturn's equator can reach 1,000 miles per hour. And the *Voyagers* discovered wild, swirling storms, like those in Jupiter's atmosphere.

Saturn's famous rings are made up of countless pieces of rock and ice in orbit around the planet. If you could scoop up all the particles in the rings, you would have enough rock and ice to make a medium-sized moon. Scientists think that the rings may be what's left of a moon that was shattered by collisions.

The *Voyagers* were also part of an experiment to learn more about the rings. Scientists had the spacecraft send radio signals that would have to pass through the rings on the way back to Earth. The radio signals changed a little bit as they went through the rings. By studying these changes, scientists learned that the pieces of rock and ice that make up Saturn's rings come in many different sizes. Some are as small as grains of sand. Some are as big as trucks.

▲ ▶ Saturn's rings. Colors have been added to the photographs by a computer to show different parts of the rings.

◄ This picture shows Saturn, its rings, and two of its moons, Tethys and Dione.

From Earth, Saturn appears to have three broad rings. The *Voyagers'* pictures seemed to show thousands and thousands of rings. Other instruments on the two spacecraft showed that the rings are all part of a huge sheet of particles. There are no completely empty gaps. The thin sheet starts close to Saturn's cloud tops and stretches out 40,000 miles. Three very faint rings orbit outside the main sheet.

The *Voyagers* discovered a very small moon, invisible from Earth, at the outer edge of the main sheet of rings. This moon, like the rings themselves, is probably a piece of a larger moon that was shattered when it was hit by a comet or asteroid. There are other small moons like this one that help shape the rings and sweep the edges clean.

The solar system can be a dangerous place! One of Saturn's moons, Mimas, barely survived a colossal collision. The collision left an enormous crater 80 miles wide, with a mountain at its center that is higher than Mount Everest. If the collision had been much harder, Mimas would have split apart.

Mimas

Another moon, Hyperion, is probably a piece of what was once a larger moon that did break apart.

Hyperion

Most of Saturn's moons are icy balls that were formed at the same time as the planet. But Phoebe is different. It is probably an asteroid that came too close to Saturn and was captured by the pull of the planet's gravity. The photograph is blurry because Phoebe is small and *Voyager* was far away.

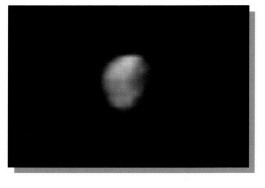
Phoebe

Titan, Saturn's largest moon, fascinated scientists. Before the *Voyager* mission, it was the only moon in the solar system known to have an atmosphere. From Earth, scientists had detected methane gas around Titan, but they could not tell whether there were other gases in its atmosphere. Scientists sent *Voyager* 1 on a path that took it very close to this unusual moon so they could learn more about it.

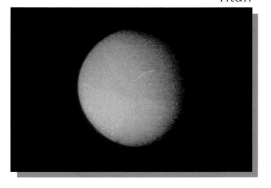
Titan

When the spacecraft arrived at Titan, it found a thick orange haze covering the moon. Titan's atmosphere is very thick—more than one and a half times as thick as the air on Earth. It is made up mostly of nitrogen gas, just like Earth's atmosphere. But unlike the air we breathe, Titan's air has no oxygen in it.

What is below the orange haze? *Voyager* 1's cameras could not see to Titan's surface, but its other instruments sent back clues. The chemical ethane is as abundant on Titan as water is on Earth. Scientists think that there might be ethane rainstorms, and maybe even ethane rivers and ethane lakes on this distant moon.

Because *Voyager* 1's path took it so close to Titan, it was not able to go on to Uranus and Neptune. Instead, the spacecraft headed up and out of the main plane of the solar system.

Voyager 2 was on a path that allowed it to visit the last two giant planets. Using Saturn's gravity like a giant slingshot, *Voyager* 2 said good-bye to its twin and headed to Uranus alone.

◄ This photograph of Titan's hazy orange atmosphere was taken from a distance of 270,000 miles.

URANUS

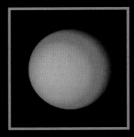

Uranus is so far away that it took *Voyager* 2 more than four years to travel there from Saturn. The spacecraft was still 150 million miles away when it took this picture.

Because Uranus is so far from the Sun, it does not get much heat or light. It is a cold, dark planet. Taking pictures at Uranus is like taking pictures at twilight on Earth. As *Voyager* 2 approached Uranus, scientists had to adjust its cameras to take photographs in this dim light.

The spacecraft got closer and closer to the planet, but all the pictures relayed back to Earth looked the same. Uranus' pale blue atmosphere was almost featureless. It does not have streaming bands of color or swirling storms like the atmospheres of Jupiter and Saturn. *Voyager* did measure strong winds, but they were not as strong as the winds on the other two planets.

Uranus' atmosphere is made up mostly of hydrogen and helium gas, like the atmospheres of Jupiter and Saturn. But it also has small amounts of methane. It is the methane that gives Uranus its blue color.

Although this pale blue planet looks calm and peaceful, scientists think it had a violent past. Early in its history, Uranus was probably hit by a huge object, maybe a comet the size of Earth. The collision was so violent that Uranus was knocked over. Now the planet lies on its side. As it orbits around the Sun, first its south pole then its north pole point toward the Sun.

The same year that the *Voyagers* were launched, scientists looking through telescopes on Earth discovered nine narrow rings around Uranus. When *Voyager* 2 arrived at the planet 9 years later, it found two more.

Early in Uranus' history a huge asteroid or comet may have knocked it onto its side. When *Voyager* 2 arrived in 1986 it approached the planet's south pole.

▶ Colors have been added to this picture of Uranus by a computer to show the planet's temperature. Areas near the south pole, shown in yellow and orange, were warmer at the time of *Voyager's* approach because they were facing the Sun.

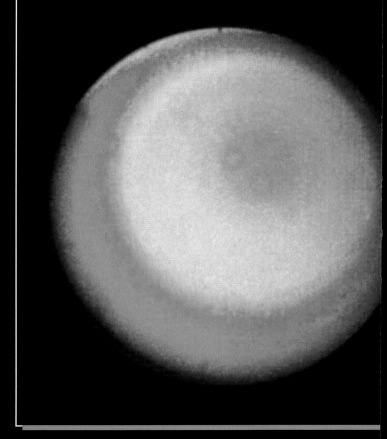

Uranus' rings are very different from both the faint ring around Jupiter and the broad sheet of rings around Saturn. The rings of Jupiter and Saturn have many tiny particles in them. Uranus' rings seem to be made up mostly of big chunks of rock and ice the size of boulders. Several clues suggest that the rings might be much younger than Uranus. A missing moon, maybe broken apart by an impact, might have disintegrated to form the chunky rings.

The rings are also much darker than those of Jupiter and Saturn. The boulders in Uranus' rings are as black as charcoal.

The picture below, and a picture like it from Saturn, gave scientists a clue to the mystery of what holds a ring together. Because of *Voyager*'s photographs, scientists now know that particles can be held in the shape of a ring by two small moons, one on each side of the ring. Each moon's gravity pulls on the particles in a kind of tug-of-war, which keeps the particles in a ring between them.

The *Voyagers* showed that moons and rings are closely related. Not only can rings be held in place by small moons, but the rings themselves may be what's left of moons that were shattered by collisions with comets or asteroids.

▲ Uranus' rings. The two rings *Voyager* 2 discovered are so faint that they don't show up in this picture.

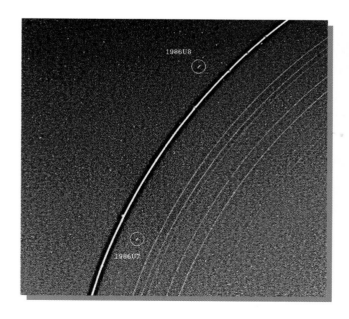

▲ Two tiny moons (*circled*), close to one of Uranus' rings.

Before *Voyager* 2 visited Uranus, astronomers had found five moons around the planet. They did not know how big these moons were, or what they were made of. In just a few hours, *Voyager* discovered ten new moons. It found that Uranus' moons are made mostly of ice and rock, and that even its largest moons, Titania and Oberon, are only half the size of Earth's moon.

Miranda is the closest moon to the planet. It looks like a giant jigsaw puzzle whose pieces were scrambled. Part of its surface looks old and cratered, and part of it looks young and very rough. There are ice cliffs ten miles high and canyons ten miles deep. Scientists now think that partially melted ice pushes its way to the surface, creating Miranda's patchwork appearance.

Titania

Oberon

Miranda

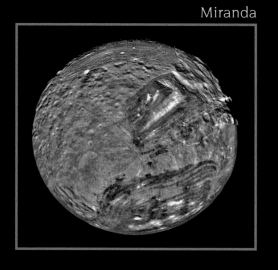

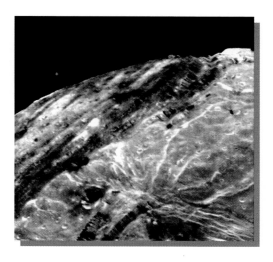

▲ Part of Miranda's surface.

Voyager 2 flew past Uranus very quickly. Most pictures of the planet, its rings, and its moons were taken in only six hours. But those six hours gave scientists their first real look at this pale blue planet.

After traveling nearly 3 billion miles, *Voyager* still had 1 1/2 billion miles to go before reaching Neptune, the last giant planet in our solar system.

◄ *Voyager* 2 looked back to take this farewell photograph of Uranus from a distance of 600,000 miles.

Voyager 2 had been traveling for 12 years. The aging spacecraft had survived its long trip through space and was finally nearing Neptune. There was great excitement in Mission Control. Scientists had waited a long time for a close look at this mysterious planet.

Voyager did not disappoint them. The very first close-up pictures revealed a moon that had never been seen before. It was small, dark, bumpy, and orbiting very close to Neptune. The moon looked as if it had lived through many collisions. *Voyager* 2 would discover five more small moons before it left Neptune.

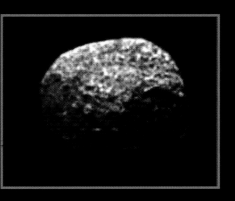

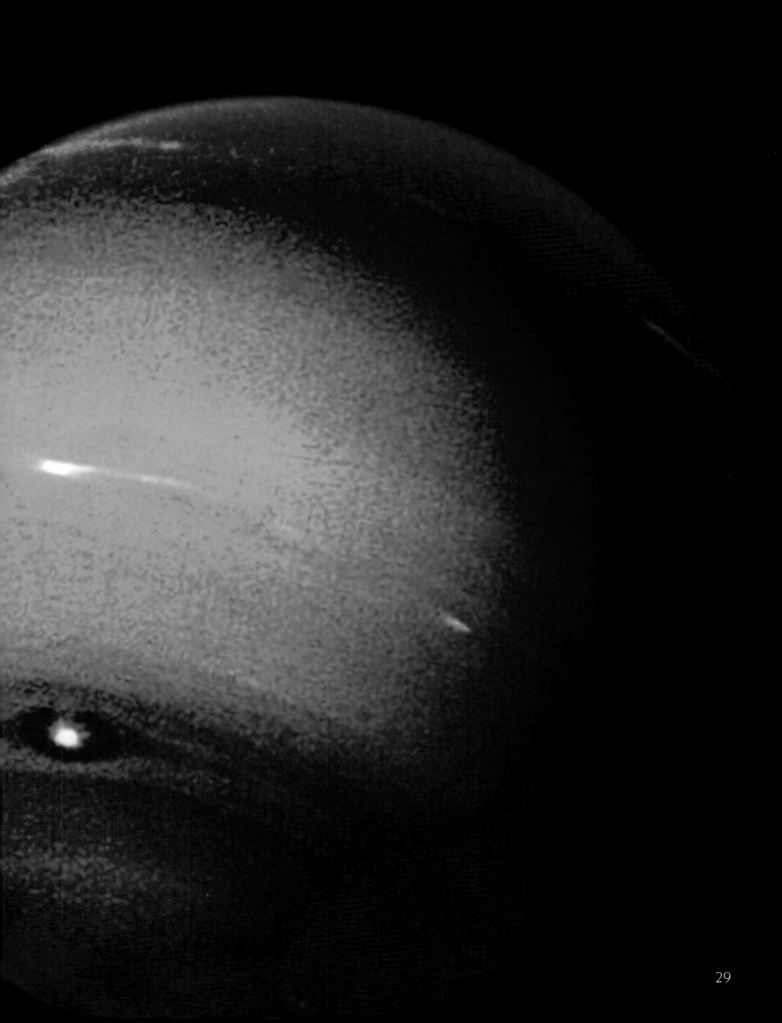

Voyager's next pictures brought another discovery: there are rings around this planet, too. Two are narrow, and two are broad. The particles that make up Neptune's rings are small, like those of Jupiter's rings. But they are also very black, like the boulders circling Uranus.

Neptune's rings are unusual because some parts of them are thicker than others. The particles in the rings are not spread out evenly. Scientists think that the dust in the rings could be kept in clumps by the pull of two small moons.

Scientists expected Neptune to be a lot like Uranus because the two planets are about the same size and are very, very far away from the Sun. But *Voyager*'s pictures surprised them. Neptune's atmosphere has wild storms, like those on Jupiter and Saturn. This cold, blue planet has violent weather.

One huge storm was named the Great Dark Spot because it reminded scientists of Jupiter's Great Red Spot. Winds near its edges are the strongest measured on any planet—over 1,400 miles per hour!

▼ Two photographs were combined to make this picture of Neptune's rings.

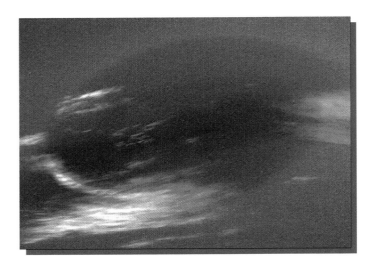

▲ A close-up picture of the Great Dark Spot.

▶ A more distant view of Neptune, showing the Great Dark Spot and a smaller storm to the south.

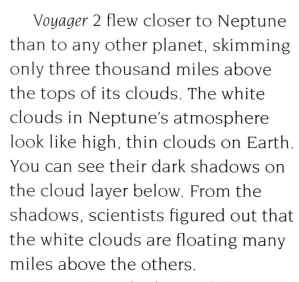

Voyager 2 flew closer to Neptune than to any other planet, skimming only three thousand miles above the tops of its clouds. The white clouds in Neptune's atmosphere look like high, thin clouds on Earth. You can see their dark shadows on the cloud layer below. From the shadows, scientists figured out that the white clouds are floating many miles above the others.

Voyager's path also took it very close to Neptune's rings. As it passed the rings, it was hit again and again by tiny dust particles. Even though the particles were very small, they were moving so fast that *Voyager* could have been damaged. But the bombardment lasted only a few moments, and the little spacecraft made it safely past. *Voyager* 2 raced toward its last target, Neptune's largest moon, Triton.

Very little was known about Triton, but observations from Earth led scientists to believe that it might have an atmosphere. *Voyager* 2 found that it does. Triton's atmosphere is made up of the same gases—nitrogen and methane—as the atmosphere of Saturn's moon, Titan. But Triton's atmosphere is very, very thin. *Voyager*'s cameras could easily see through it to the moon's surface.

Most moons are formed with their planet, so they orbit in the same direction as the planet spins. Triton orbits Neptune in the "wrong" direction. This makes scientists think that Triton was formed somewhere else in the solar system but came too close to Neptune and was captured by the planet's gravity.

After Triton was captured, the forces pulling it toward Neptune may have heated the moon and melted it. It is possible that for a billion years Triton was a liquid moon. Today, Triton is the coldest place in the solar system—its temperature is 390 degrees Fahrenheit below zero. Its surface is completely frozen.

Triton

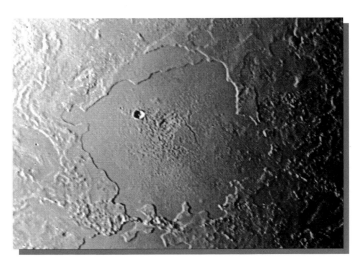

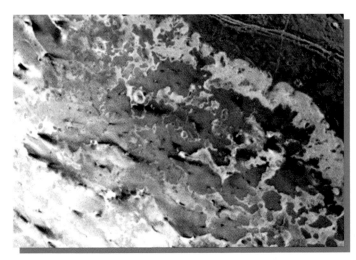

▲ *Center*: Part of Triton's surface. The distance across the photograph is about 300 miles. *Bottom*: Part of the ice cap at Triton's south pole. The dark smudges may be ice geysers.

Parts of Triton are covered by ice caps. At first, scientists couldn't explain the dark streaks they saw against the pale ice. But as they looked at more pictures, they saw that dark jets of ice and gas were shooting up from the surface and then were being carried sideways by the wind. These jets, called geysers, occur when liquid below the surface explodes up through weak spots in the ice—like a warm soft drink when you pop open the can. Some geysers may erupt for months, spraying ice and gas miles into Triton's thin atmosphere and leaving dark streaks on its icy surface.

Ice geysers had never been seen before. This discovery, on the coldest moon in the solar system, was an exciting end to a 12-year adventure. Three days after leaving Triton, Voyager 2 was 3 million miles from the moon. As it sped away, it gave scientists this last look at Neptune and Triton. It was not long before the last giant planet was just a dot in the distance.

◀ Voyager's last look at Neptune and Triton.

The *Voyagers* are still traveling.

Since leaving Saturn, *Voyager* 1 has been heading north out of the solar system. *Voyager* 2 is now heading south. Although the *Voyagers* are no longer taking pictures, they are still collecting data. They will continue to send information back to Earth until about the year 2020. Both spacecraft are studying the solar wind, high energy particles that stream out of the Sun. And they are searching for the edge of the solar system—the place where our Sun's influence ends.

The *Voyagers* won't stop there. They will continue on into the empty space between the stars. Although they are traveling at more than 35,000 miles per hour, neither spacecraft will come near another star for thousands and thousands of years.

It is very unlikely that either *Voyager* will be found by space travelers from another world. But just in case, each carries a message from its home planet. A copper record attached to the side of each spacecraft contains pictures and sounds from Earth. It begins:

"This is a present from a small and distant world,

a token of our sounds, our science, our images,

our music, our thoughts, and our feelings."

The *Voyagers* are still traveling, heading toward the stars, carrying a message from all of us.

▶ The record attached to each *Voyager* contains greetings in more than 60 languages, music from many different cultures, and other sounds from the Earth, such as the songs of humpback whales. The record's cover (*inset*) has symbols showing where Earth is located in the universe.

The Giant Planets Today

The *Voyagers* completed their remarkable tour of Jupiter, Saturn, Uranus, and Neptune more than 15 year ago. Their amazing discoveries changed what we know about the giant planets, their moons and rings.

Since the *Voyager* mission, two other spacecraft have visited the outer solar system.

The *Galileo* spacecraft arrived at Jupiter in 1995. It explored the planet and its odd assortment of moons for almost 8 years. *Galileo* confirmed what the *Voyagers'* suspected—Europa's icy surface hides an ocean of water! It also found hints of salty oceans beneath the surfaces of two other moons, Callisto and Ganymede.

In 2004, the *Cassini* spacecraft arrived at Saturn. It settled into orbit to study the planet and its magnificent rings. *Cassini* even dropped a small probe into Titan's hazy orange atmosphere. The *Huygens* probe drifted down to Titan's soggy surface. It sent back the first photos of the moon's hidden landscape.

The *Voyagers'* stunning photographs showed that our solar system is much more interesting and beautiful than anyone imagined.

The chart on the next page shows what we know about the giant planets today and compares them to our own planet.

An active volcano on Jupiter's moon, Io. The orange area on the left is flowing lava. (*Galileo*)

A close-up of Europa's icy surface. (*Galileo*)

Saturn's tiny moon, Phoebe, seen close-up for the first time. (*Cassini*)

Planet	Average Distance from Sun (AU) [1]	Diameter (miles)	Diameter [2] (in Earth diameters)	Composition	Known Moons	Rings	Orbital Period [3] (Earth years)
Earth	1	7,926	1	Rocks, metals	1	0	1
Jupiter	5.2	88,846	11.2	Hydrogen, helium, hydrogen compounds	63	1	11.9
Saturn	9.5	74,900	9.5	Hydrogen, helium, hydrogen compounds	33	1,000s	29.4
Uranus	19.2	31,763	4	Hydrogen, helium, hydrogen compounds	27	11	84
Neptune	30.1	30,775	3.9	Hydrogen, helium, hydrogen compounds	14	5	164.8

[1] AU = astronomical unit. The distance between the Earth and the Sun, or about 93 million miles. This means, for example, that Jupiter is 5.2 times farther from the Sun than the Earth is.

[2] Diameter in Earth Diameters. Earth's diameter is 7,926 miles. Jupiter's diameter is 88,846 miles or 11.2 times Earth's diameter.

[3] Orbital Period. The amount of time it takes a planet to travel once around the Sun.

Glossary

asteroids: Small rocky objects that orbit the Sun. Thousands of asteroids orbit in a region called the asteroid belt, which lies between the orbits of Mars and Jupiter. However, some have been found in other orbits, including some that cross Earth's orbit.

asteroid belt: The region between the orbits of Mars and Jupiter where most asteroids are found.

astronomer: A scientist who studies the planets, stars, galaxies, and other astronomical objects.

atmosphere: A layer of gas surrounding a planet or moon, held in place by the force of gravity.

crater: A bowl-shaped depression on the surface of a planet or moon caused by the impact of another body such as an asteroid or comet.

crust: The relatively thin, solid outer layer of a terrestrial planet or moon.

ethane: A colorless, odorless gas made of carbon and hydrogen.

Fahrenheit: A temperature scale. On this scale, the freezing point of water is 32°F, the boiling point of water is 212°F, and the interval between is divided into 180 equal parts called degrees Fahrenheit.

giant planets: Jupiter, Saturn, Uranus, and Neptune. They are called the giant planets because they are so much larger than the other planets in the solar system.

gravity: The attractive force that any object with mass has on all other objects with mass. The greater the mass of the object, the stronger its gravitational pull.

interstellar: The space between stars in a galaxy.

lava: Molten rock that has risen through a planet's crust and spilled onto the surface.

meteorite: A chunk of rock or metal that strikes the surface of a planet or moon.

methane: A colorless, odorless gas made of carbon and hydrogen.

moon: A small body in orbit around a planet.

nitrogen gas: A colorless, odorless gas made of two nitrogen atoms. It makes up 78 percent of Earth's atmosphere.

orbit: The path of one body around another, as a result of the force of gravity between them. Examples are a planet's path around the Sun and a moon's path around a planet.

planet: In our solar system, one of the nine major bodies that orbit the Sun. More generally, a celestial body that orbits a star and is big enough that its gravity has pulled it into a spherical shape.

radar: Acronym for RAdio Detection And Ranging. A radar bounces radio waves off a distant object, then receives and analyzes the reflected waves to determine the location and speed of the object.

solar wind: A stream of high-energy particles that flows outward from the Sun into the solar system.

star: A ball of hot gas held together by its gravity and generating energy at its center.

telescope: An instrument used to collect and focus light to produce a magnified image of a faraway object.

Index

About the Authors

SALLY RIDE has been interested in science since she was a child. She earned bachelor's degrees in physics and English and a Ph.D. in physics from Stanford University. In 1983 she became the first American woman to fly in space, when she made a six-day flight aboard the space shuttle *Challenger*. She made her second trip into space in 1984. Dr. Ride is now a professor of physics at the University of California, San Diego. She is also founder of Sally Ride Science, a company that creates events, programs and publications for young people interested in science.

TAM O'SHAUGHNESSY and Sally Ride have been friends since they were teens competing in junior tennis tournaments. Dr. O'Shaughnessy holds a master's degree in biology and a Ph.D. in education from the University of California, Riverside. She is a professor of school psychology at San Diego State University. Tam and Sally have written three other children's science books including, *The Third Planet: Exploring The Earth From Space*. They won the American Institute of Physics 1995 Children's Science Writing Award.

To Our Fathers,
For their lifelong spirit of adventure

Copyright © 1992, 2005 by Sally Ride and Tam O'Shaughnessy

Photographs courtesy National Aeronautics and Space Administration

Cover design by Joe McClune
Illustrations by Gaylord Welker

Published by Sally Ride Science
9191 Towne Centre Drive, Suite L101, San Diego, CA 92122

Sally Ride Science is a trademark of Imaginary Lines, Inc.
SallyRideScience.com

Manufactured in the United States of America

ISBN 0-9753920-5-0 (previously ISBN 0-517-58157-4)

10 9 8 7 6 5 4 3 2 1

Second Edition